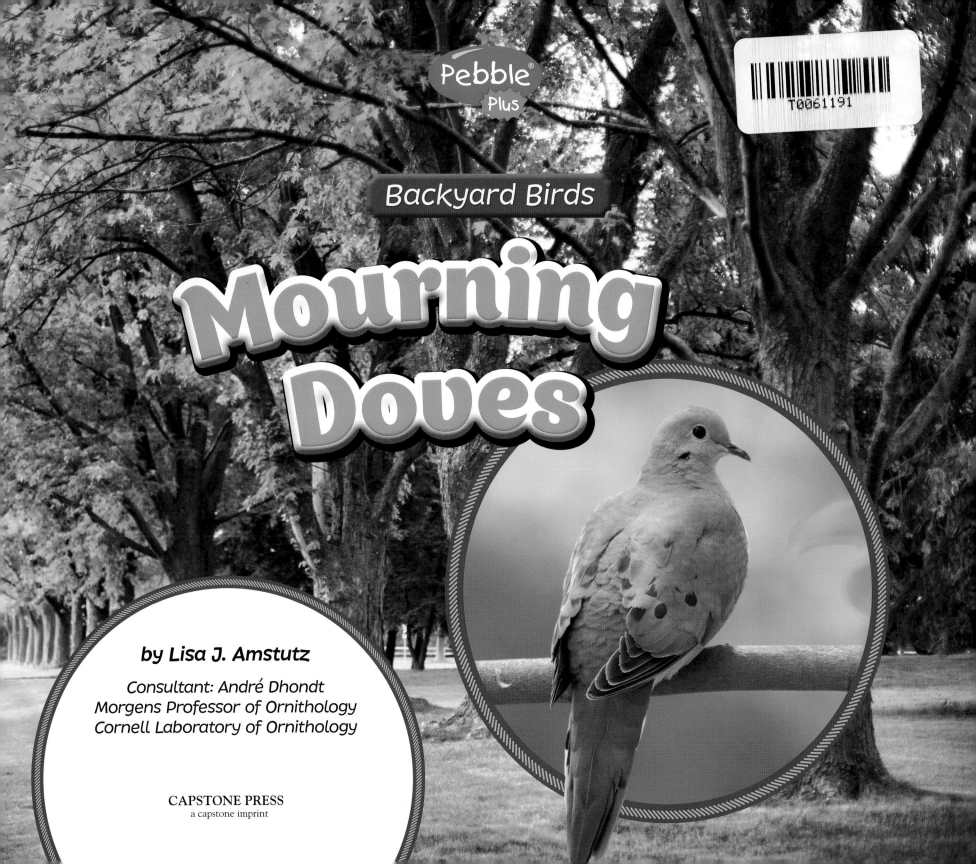

Pebble® Plus

Backyard Birds

Mourning Doves

by Lisa J. Amstutz

Consultant: André Dhondt
Morgens Professor of Ornithology
Cornell Laboratory of Ornithology

CAPSTONE PRESS
a capstone imprint

Pebble Plus is published by Capstone Press,
1710 Roe Crest Drive, North Mankato, Minnesota 56003
www.mycapstone.com

Copyright © 2016 by Capstone Press, a Capstone imprint. All rights reserved. No part
of this publication may be reproduced in whole or in part, or stored in a retrieval system, or
transmitted in any form or by any means, electronic, mechanical, photocopying, recording,
or otherwise, without written permission of the publisher.

Library of Congress Cataloging-in-Publication Data
Cataloging-in-Publication data is on file with the Library of Congress.
ISBN 978-1-4914-8514-9 (library binding)
ISBN 978-1-4914-8518-7 (paperback)
ISBN 978-1-4914-8522-4 (eBook PDF)

Editorial Credits
Nikki Bruno Clapper, editor; Katelin Plekkenpol and Juliette Peters, designers;
Jo Miller, media researcher; Tori Abraham, production specialist

Photo Credits
Alamy: Robert M. Vera, 17; Getty Images: Moment Open/loriambrosio, 19, Panoramic Images, 13;
Minden Pictures: FLPA/S & D & K Maslowski, 11; Newscom: Danita Delimont Photography/Larry
Ditto, 5; Shutterstock: Charles Brutlag, Cover (inset), 1 (inset), IrinaK, 9, Lee Prince, 15, N K, Cover
(background) 1 (background), 2-3, 24, Robert A. Mansker, 21, StevenRussellSmithPhotos, 7, Vitaly
Raduntsev, flowers (throughout)

Note to Parents and Teachers

The Backyard Birds set supports national curriculum standards for science related to
life science and ecosystems. This book describes and illustrates mourning doves. The
images support early readers in understanding the text. The repetition of words and
phrases helps early readers learn new words. This book also introduces early readers
to subject-specific vocabulary words, which are defined in the Glossary section. Early
readers may need assistance to read some words and to use the Table of Contents,
Glossary, Read More, Internet Sites, Critical Thinking Using the Common Core, and
Index sections of the book.

Printed in the United States of America in North Mankato, Minnesota.
102015   009221CGS16

Table of Contents

All About Mourning Doves

Mourning doves bob
their heads as they walk.
They call softly.
Coo, coo, coo.

An adult dove is 9 to 13 inches (23 to 33 centimeters) long. Doves have short legs. Their feathers are tan with black spots.

A mourning dove swallows
pebbles and sand called grit.
It also swallows seeds.
The grit helps grind seeds
in the bird's stomach.

Where Mourning Doves Live

Mourning doves live
in North America and
Central America. They like
open areas. Yards, fields,
and deserts are their homes.

Mourning doves build nests
with pine needles, twigs,
and grasses. Stumps or
low branches are the best
places for their nests.

The Life of a Mourning Dove

A female dove lays two eggs.

Both parents sit on the eggs

to keep them warm.

After two weeks chicks hatch.

The chicks are called squabs.

Squabs suck a liquid
called "pigeon milk" from
a parent's crop. The crop is
part of a dove's throat.

Soon the squabs will eat seeds.

Doves form flocks in fall
and winter. They watch
for predators. Cats, snakes,
and owls eat doves.
People hunt doves too.

Look for mourning

doves in your yard.

Put birdseed on the ground.

Set up a tray feeder.

Then watch them eat!

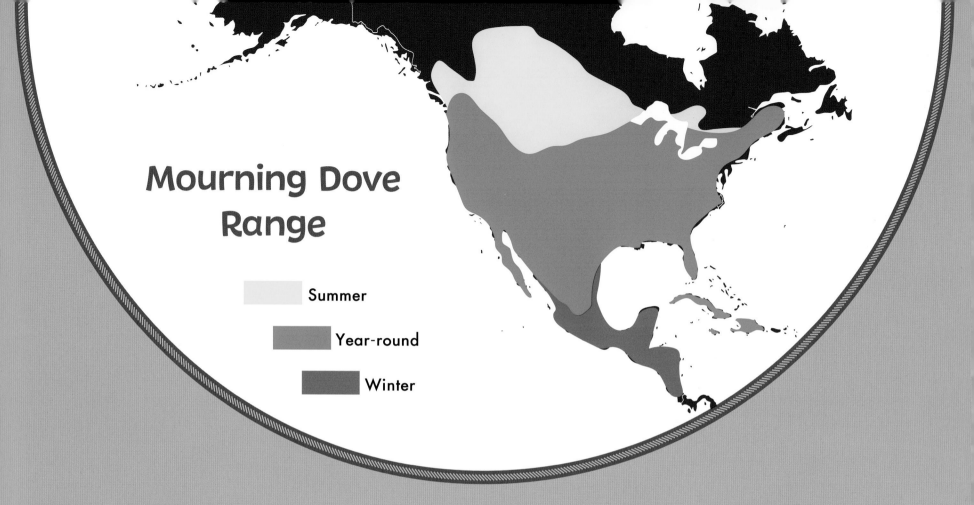

Mourning Dove Range

Summer

Year-round

Winter

Glossary

crop—a part of a bird's throat

desert—a dry area with little rain

flock—a group of the same kind of animal; members of flocks live, travel, and eat together

grit—small pieces of stone or sand; birds eat grit to help grind their food

hatch—to break out of an egg

predator—an animal that hunts other animals for food

squab—a baby dove or pigeon

Read More

Cummings, Kermit. *A Backyard Birding Adventure: What's in Your Yard?* Dallas: Brown Books Kids, 2015.

Martin, Isabel. *Birds: A Question and Answer Book.* Pebble Plus: Animal Kingdom Questions and Answers. North Mankato, Minn.: Capstone Press, 2015.

Rockwell, Lizzy. *A Bird Is a Bird.* New York: Holiday House, 2015.

Internet Sites

FactHound offers a safe, fun way to find Internet sites related to this book. All of the sites on FactHound have been researched by our staff.

Here's all you do:

Visit *www.facthound.com*

Type in this code: 9781491485149

Critical Thinking
Using the Common Core

1. What do mourning doves do to prepare for and take care of their chicks? (Key Ideas and Details)

2. What is a crop? What do adult mourning doves have in their crops? (Craft and Structure)

3. How do you think grit helps grind food? (Integration of Knowledge and Ideas)

Index